# Comple

# Guide A to Z

## Budget Friendly Guide to Buying Used Motorhome

By

# Bruce Bowers

Published by:

**Valencia Publishing House**
P.O. Box 548
Wilmer, Alabama 36587

Cover & Interior designed

By

Robin Hollman

*First Edition*

# TABLE OF CONTENTS

# I. INTRODUCTION

What do you want to do when you retire? Do you want to live off your savings and go jet-setting around the world, or lounge around in the best beaches while sipping a sweet cocktail drink? Are you a home buddy who wants to stay inside all day like a couch potato, or can you imagine yourself riding across the country in your own personalized mobile home?

Imagine this: binge-watching your favorite shows on TV and putting your feet up on your couch while cracking open a nice cold can of beer—all while traveling through all 50 states and enjoying the sights, sounds, and adventures on the road. That is the beauty and luxury of living in a mobile home, and the appeal is just too enticing for many retired Americans to resist. After all, who wouldn't want to travel the country in the comfort of their own home? I know I would!

In this in-depth guide, I will let you in on all the tips, tricks, and nitty gritty of choosing the best RV for you, so that you will get exactly your money's worth when you finally make that fated purchase. You definitely would not want to put your hard-earned money to waste—not when you've saved it all up so that you can retire comfortably in the motorhome of your choice. It is a big decision after all—one that will determine the state and quality of your retirement—which is why we will go through all the details in buying your own RV.

Excited yet? You should be!

## WHAT IS AN RV?

An RV stands for Recreational Vehicle, and this motorhome can be used both for camping and traveling and for temporary accommodation. Usually, your typical RV would also contain the basic amenities and necessities that are present in most normal houses, except that an RV is constantly mobile and on the go. You can drive the RV around with you wherever you go in a motorized variety, or an RV can also be towable, which means that you tow the RV with a car or truck to take it to different places. RVs have both luxurious models and more affordable and budget-friendly ones, and the decorations and modifications all depend on the needs of the occupants.

As with anything (and with any important purchase decision in life), you always have to prioritize your needs or purpose for buying the RV. Do you plan on living in your motorhome fulltime? Then you need to pick a layout of the RV that is well-suited to your lifestyle and your spatial requirements. While size can be the more obvious factor to consider when choosing the best motorhome for you, people often neglect the importance of layout more than the size. The layout does indeed matter more because size can often be tricky—you might buy yourself a huge and supersized trailer only to feel cramped and find it lacking inside when you are finally living in it all because of poor layout planning. Always make sure that you properly position all of the elements inside your motorhome so that you can feel like space is big and wide due to the ergonomic feel inside.

One suggestion to deal with space constraints inside a mobile home is the pullout. Typically designed to make the living room feel larger than it really is, the pullout is definitely a must-have when you want to maximize your space.

It is also fairly important to know how to live the sort of minimalist life when you choose to live permanently in a mobile home. You have to determine which luxuries in life you can live without, and which ones are absolute necessities.

Do you really need an oven, or are you good with a small microwave? Do you need a freezer or a simple fridge will do? Do you value a bathroom that is right where your bed is, or do you need the space to walk around on your bedside even more? These are crucial decisions you have to identify first before you make your purchase wantonly.

## WHAT ARE THE ADVANTAGES OF AN RV?

Aside from the fact that owning an RV is pretty much like taking your own comfy home with you wherever you go without worrying about things you might leave behind on a trip or go to the bathroom in the middle of the journey (or even wanting to stretch out, kick back, and relax on your own bed), a RV is the perfect way to go on a vacation with your family and friends.

It certainly beats spending heaps and heaps of dough just to get away, because it is inexpensive as it is comfortable and practical. Traveling around on your holiday in an RV also beats checking in to a pricey hotel with all of your family and friends, and the costs of living in a hotel for a few days are definitely way higher than renting a campsite to park your RV in.

Traveling around in your RV also means that you can even take your pets or your dog with you, and you most definitely can't do that when you're checked into a hotel or on a plane (kennel fees can be quite expensive too).

As for the food, you can save tons of bucks just by cooking your own food rather than ordering the ridiculously expensive plated meals outside in restaurants and hotel lobbies.

You can choose however way you want to cook your food, whether you're on a strict diet or just want to experience the warm comfort of a home-cooked meal.

You can set up a campfire and roast up a storm, or set up a grill and have a blast with your barbecue. You can stock up on snacks in your own pantry instead of desperately looking around for a supermarket to buy your chips and drinks when your tummy is grumpy and grumbling, and in case you do get a case of the munchies, you can even snack any time you want to.

On extremely uncomfortable emergency cases of the upset stomach, you don't even have to put up with dingy public bathrooms to do the deed. You can go comfortably and in your own pace inside your own bathroom—and you don't even have to worry about cleanliness and sanitation because you are following your own basic personal hygiene inside your RV. And if you are feeling a little grimy and want to be instantly refreshed, go take a cold or hot shower at any time!

When you are traveling across the country in an RV, you can also basically take whatever you want with you on the road without worrying about what you might have left behind. You can take supplies, spare materials, toys and games for the bored kids, and lots of indoor entertainment for when the weather outside isn't cooperating too well. You can also skip the planning on your outfit for all those days of travel as you will be bringing your whole wardrobe along with you! You can even have your bikes tag along on the trip with you and load them onto the vehicle at the back of the RV or inside. The possibilities are totally endless.

## WHAT ARE THE DISADVANTAGES OF AN RV?

If it sounds too good to be true, that's because there are pros and always cons to every single venture. If you do not have enough space to store your RV when it is not being used, where will you park it semi-permanently?

There are some places where you can rent a space for you to store your RV when it is not in use, but these storage fees can be quite expensive. On top of that, maintenance fees and costs can also skyrocket, especially if you don't want your RV to break down unexpectedly in dreaded remote areas.

Parts for the RV are usually more expensive than typical car parts as they are more specialized, so you have to take maintenance and repair costs into consideration all the time.

Another major thing to consider when you are traveling in your RV is that you need to factor in the height of your motorhome. The vehicle might have a height that does not provide enough clearance when you are passing under a bridge, and underneath a bridge is not a good place to get stuck. It will not only cost you loads of cash and compromise your safety during your trip, but it will also most definitely ruin your supposedly enjoyable holiday vacation.

The biggest thing to consider when traveling using your mobile home is the whopping fuel cost for long distances. That is, after all, what you are paying for to get all of the comfort and luxury of a motorhome. There is also the time factor, as traveling in an RV is definitely much slower than flying to a destination via an airplane.

You also have to learn how to clean up after yourself, as there will be no room service and no bellhops to attend to you and be at your service at your beck and call.

Make sure you keep all of these different factors in mind before you buy your mobile home! If you are still feeling iffy about it, why not go for a test run?

You can opt for a trial of the lifestyle by renting an RV first before you make your big purchase. There are many options to rent a motorhome during a short holiday vacation just so you can get the feel of living in it before buying one permanently.

You can compare your trip with your previous trips and factor in all the details and elements of the journey to see if living in a motorhome is really the best choice for you.

# III. TYPES OF RVS AND MOTORHOMES

Now that we've tackled the different factors to consider and the pros and cons of buying and living in an RV, you need to know about the different types—because boy, are there a lot! Before you make the big decision, you should know how to find and buy the right type, the different varieties for different uses, the features of each, as well as the advantages and disadvantages of every single one. It might sound completely overwhelming especially for the anxious and tentative beginner, but that's what I'm here for, right? Don't fret—this guide definitely has you covered!

## THE TWO BASIC TYPES OF RVS

As we have mentioned before, typical RVs can be categorized into two major varieties: the drivable ones, and the towable ones. There are different classes within each variety, and the price range also differs greatly from those that are easy on the wallet to those that will break your bank. You should always keep in mind how often you will be using your RV. For instance, some campers normally just use their mobile homes whenever they go camping once in a while, but some retirees love to hit the open road and live in their mobile homes forever, going cross-country on a daily basis. Just bear in mind that the more comfortable and the higher the level the luxury of your mobile home is, the higher the price tag will be as well, so always be wary of that so that you won't get a heart attack with the shock of the costs.

It is also important to note that there are such things as Toy Trailers, and no, these aren't the ones that your kids love to bang against each other in the playroom. Toy Trailers are generally still classified as Recreational Vehicles, but their purpose is more for the transport of so-called "toys" such as motorbikes, quad bikes, racing cars, bicycles, rafts, boats, and even ATVs. Because the function of these Toy Trailers is generally to transport these recreational "toys," the living spaces within them can be quite small compared to regular camping RVs.

Sometimes, there are single-story buses or double-story buses that owners like to remodel into RVs. They are refitted based on an individual's particular traveling needs, but this kind of customization can take a long time and can get very expensive. Maintenance can also be pretty heavy on the wallet, and some campsites might not allow them to park as they do not look like RVs.

## TOWABLE RECREATIONAL VEHICLES

With towable recreational vehicles, you can separate your driving area from your main living area, making it easy and convenient for when you want to drive around without having to carry your whole home with you wherever you go.

You can also choose to sell one part and retain the other part, as both areas are completely separate and independent from each other. Plus, the towable RV has no mechanical parts or engines that can malfunction, giving it a higher value as it can hold its price better in the market.

When you are performing regular maintenance on the towing vehicle, you can do so separately at your local garage, as oil changes and the like do not really need any specialized equipment for maintenance.

The whole trailer can be left settled and comfy at a campsite as you get your tow vehicle prepped and fixed until it is good as new. As such, the operating costs of towable recreational vehicles are much less than with an RV that's drivable.

However, there is a great deal of stiffness in the whole thing. It can be quite a big challenge to reverse and park the vehicle as there is a lack of maneuverability, and mastering the art of driving the thing around can take some time and some practiced skill.

Normally, two people are required for when you are setting up to get to the campsite, so there are cons to owning a towable RV too.

# The Different Types of RVs

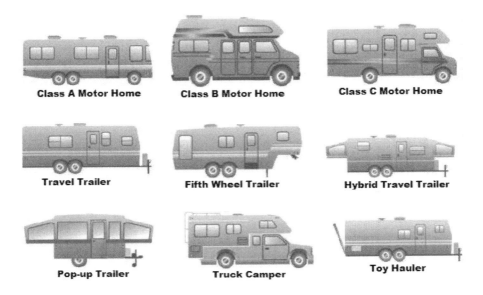

Class A Motor Home    Class B Motor Home    Class C Motor Home

Travel Trailer    Fifth Wheel Trailer    Hybrid Travel Trailer

Pop-up Trailer    Truck Camper    Toy Hauler

## TRAVEL TRAILERS

As the top-selling RV in the marketplace right now, the travel trailer has a length of about 10 feet up to 35 feet, and can sometimes have a slide out that can go for approximately three feet. These types of RVs can be very easy to set up and dismantle, which is probably the reason why these travel trailers are so popular in the industry.

Travel trailers need to be pulled along by an independent vehicle equipped with load distributing hitches so that the trailer can be controlled while moving.

With a 125 volt electrical system, travel trailers have a refrigerator, a toilet, decent cooking facilities, faucets, sinks, a shower, water tanks for both fresh and waste water, gas supply, and heating and air conditioning.

It can sleep up to eight people comfortably, with an option to attach a side tent to increase the floor area.

Folding camping trailers can be cheapest of all the mobile homes in the industry mainly because these collapsible trailers or pop-ups are very lightweight. If you and your friends and family are the types of campers who prefer not to sleep on the ground, folding camping trailers are your best bet.

Easy to set up at camping sites, folding camping trailers can have one or two folding outsides that can open up the trailer, with options for expandable tents with fabric tops or solid roofs. For families with limited storage space, this type of small RV can be very efficient.

It can have an ice box, a refrigerator, water tanks, heating, cooking facilities, and a propane gas supply. They can sleep up to six people, with a price range of $4000 to $25,000.

Just like the name suggests, fifth wheelers have an extension over the tow vehicle at the front of the box for support, and as such, not all kinds of vehicles can tow this mobile home. The front area can serve as an extra bedroom for the vehicle, and a fifth wheel can have slide outs to expand the floor space. In fact, slide outs can be as many as five, so there is a great deal of opportunity for expansion here.

It has heating and air conditioners, a refrigerator, a kitchen, water tanks for both fresh, grey, and black water, a self-contained shower and toilet, a sink, a faucet, gas supply, and electrical supply.

There is also a huge window toward the back so that you and your family and friends can enjoy the beautiful panoramic view of the countryside as you go on your road adventure. Sometimes, you might need to secure an additional non-commercial driver's license in some states in order to drive a fifth wheeler, especially if the fifth wheeler exceeds set weight limits.

## TRUCK CAMPERS

Loaded onto the back of a pickup truck is a camper body for truck campers, and it can be pretty economical to drive around with because it is so compact. It is especially efficient on windy roads and uneven terrain because of the size of the truck. The rear of the truck is the access point, and despite being quite basic, a truck camper can have heating, air conditioning, a fridge, cooking facilities, and sometimes even a water tank and a toilet. It can also have an electrical system as well as gas and can sleep up to six people.

You might want to check vertical clearances of areas you will pass by before your trip because low bridges and tree branches might get in the way of the high truck. Still, truck campers are cheap, easy to buy, and even easier to store, so it remains to be one of the more economical choices for some RV aficionados.

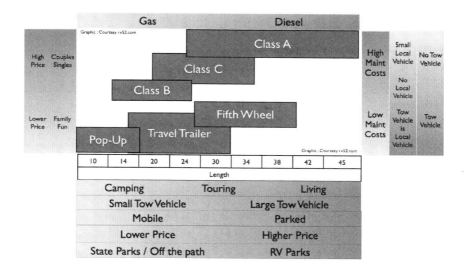

# DRIVABLE RECREATIONAL VEHICLES

While the vehicle is moving, one of the biggest advantages of having a drivable recreational vehicle is that the people inside can move around freely and be able to do the shared driving. This is a big advantage as the driver can actually get some rest and even a good night's sleep, especially during particularly long trips.

Passengers can rest or go to the toilet at any point in time during the drive, and in case of an emergency, the ignition is always ready and just within reach.

Still, having a drivable RV means that it is big and bulky and difficult to store. It takes up a lot of space and may even occupy your whole driveway. It also becomes very limited in terms of usage, as it can only ever be used for holiday vacations as it is not detachable like the towable RV.

Weighing anywhere from 15,000 to 30,000 pounds, drivable RVs have lengths ranging from 30 to 40 feet.

CLASS A

The Class A type is the top range of motorhomes, and this is because Class A RVs have practically everything you might need in a comfortable mobile home. They can come equipped with superior cooking facilities, water tanks, heating and cooling, refrigerators, faucets, toilets, sinks, showers, dryers, and even washers. Normally, one side (at the very least, or two sides) can slide out at the touch of a button to provide an additional floor space.

A bus chassis or a heavy-duty motor chassis is usually used and can perform dismally when it comes to fuel economy. A smooth and often stable drive, the Class A drivable RV has a propane gas supply, a full range of entertainment equipment, fully-equipped appliances, and a 125 electrical system.

Naturally, because of all of these top of the line features and the luxurious space of the bedrooms (some can sleep up to eight people and can have king-sized beds), the Class A drivable RV has one of the most expensive price ranges among all the other recreational vehicles. They can basically be a complete substitute for actual brick and mortar homes, what with all of the fully furnished gadgets that come with them. Of course, because of the significant size of these RVs, it is often not too practical to move them around too much. Maintenance price tags can be extremely hefty because when these things break down, it can be quite a challenge to have them fixed as parts are not too commonly available and in stock in most repair shops.

Some parts need to be ordered by special order, so it takes some time and can incur additional fees just to have those parts delivered properly.

## CLASS B

Normally, Class B drivable RVs are the smallest fully enclosed types of mobile homes, and as such, they can sometimes be called van conversions. You can definitely stand inside the van as the roof is high enough, but showers and toilets are often combined into a single space. There are no slide outs, so that alone reduces the space of the Class B RV when compared to the Class A RV. You can, however, hook up a tent onto one side so that you can at least get some extra space extension.

Small and efficient, Class B motorhomes are versatile and more economical due to its size (less than 20 feet), its weight (approximately 8000 pounds), and its fuel economy with a gas supply and 12V DC electrical outlets. It is extremely easy to park and drive around with and can fit through spaces like a normal car as well as pass under bridges without you having to worry about vertical clearances.

There is a basic kitchen with sinks and faucets, decent cooking facilities, an icebox, a refrigerator, a fresh water tank, a waste water tank, a self-contained shower and toilet, and fold out beds. It does, however, have a hard time accommodating more than four people, as it can get pretty crowded if you are planning a long getaway with a bunch of family members and friends out on the road.

## CLASS C

The Class C motorhome can be considered as the mini version of the bigger Class A RV because they are smaller in size but can be more luxurious than the Class B RV. As such, the Class C RV can be a sort of hybrid or mix of the Class A and the Class B.

There is an "over the cab" sleeping area, with a second bedroom in the back area. It can go for about 20 to 30 feet and 12,000 pounds and can come equipped with heating and air-conditioning, cooking facilities, faucets, sinks, refrigerators, toilets, fresh water tanks, waste water tanks, propane gas, electrical supplies, entertainment features, and appliances.

You can sleep up to ten people here.

# IV. FEATURES OF DIFFERENT TYPES AND FACTORS TO CONSIDER

## SPECIFIC TYPES OF RV'S

### MOTORHOMES

The most popular kind of all the units in the Recreational Vehicle industry, these are usually the biggest, the most spacious, and are also the most expensive. We've just talked about the different Classes (A, B, and C), and the pros and cons as well.

## TOTER HOME

Fully loaded from top to bottom, toter homes can be the most expensive motorhomes in the world. They can even cost around half a million dollars and are basically houses on wheels.

## DIESEL PUSHERS

The engines for diesel pushers are on the rear, and if you are looking to live life fully on the road, these inexpensive RVs are right for you.

## TRAVEL TRAILERS

If you are just a beginner RV enthusiast, travel trailers can be the perfect trial run as they range from small sizes to big sizes, and can allow you to hit the road even if you are on a tight budget.

## EXPANDABLE TRAVEL TRAILERS

Expandable travel trailers are a sort of cross between typical travel trailers and the pop-up campers out there. Once you park your expandable travel trailer, you can set up some pop-up accessories and add-ons to expand your camp or mobile home, allowing you to settle for consecutive months in a single trip.

## ICE FISHING RVS

If you have an old travel trailer and can salvage pretty much a bunch of stuff from it, you can fashion yourself an ice fishing RV. This type of motorhome features a hole over ice so that you can go fishing with your trailer.

## AIRSTREAM

An extremely popular RV brand, the Airstream is usually featured in movies and TV shows and can even have a certain cult following. It is an iconic classic where you will not go wrong with your purchase.

## WINNEBAGO

Speaking of an iconic classic, the Winnebago is the modern pioneer of motorhomes in the market. The brand itself has become a household name, and they have different types available for purchase as well.

## FACTORS TO CONSIDER WHEN BUYING YOUR RV

Aside from the typical aesthetics that you might want to consider, you should also factor in the main reason why you are buying an RV before you actually take the plunge. Who are you buying your RV for, and what are the various destinations you plan to travel to when you finally buy it? You should also know which type of RV you prefer, whether it is towable or drivable.

Finally, you should be able to differentiate between the features and amenities that you want and those that you absolutely need on your travels.

While buying an RV for yourself means that you have the ultimate power to customize your motorhome however way you want to (it IS your own mobile home, after all), you still have to consider which factors and features are customizable and can be added later on and which ones are basic and can no longer be changed along the way.

You should also consider that if you are thinking of getting yourself a towable RV, you might have to invest in an additional vehicle that can tow your motorhome. For instance, you will have to buy a truck or an SUV to tow your RV, if you don't already have a good and functioning one at home.

You should always factor in this additional expense to your budget before you make the big decision.

## FINANCIAL DECISIONS AND FINANCING INTERESTS

Making choices before you purchase your RV doesn't just include the decisions you need to make regarding the type of motorhome that you want to buy. It also means knowing how to finance your RV properly, so you need to work out your budget even before you settle on a decision. There are a variety of reliable, trustworthy, and accredited lenders that most RV dealers can offer to finance with.

Alternatively, you can take out a car loan from a third party entity or form your own bank to help you with the financing depending on your credit score, the budget for down payment, and so on. Just be wary that financing through a third party lender can sometimes yield a higher interest rate, while financing through your bank or your dealer will usually have lower interest rates.

Remember to be consistent with your monthly payments, and, if possible, choose the shorter terms of payment so that you can pay off the whole thing earlier.

Keep in mind that interest rates change quite often, so RV finance rates will follow if the prime rate increases or decreases. RV lenders and dealers normally watch each other with close proximity, so they normally follow suit once a dealer or lender adjusts its rates. They can vary from a quarter to a half point with one another.

If a used RV is about 3 years old and above, the interest rate will be higher than a brand new unit.

Down payments affect interest rates as well (10% to 20% down payments in cash or trade-in form), and so does the term of the loan. The longer the term is, the lower the interest rate. The lower the dollar amount financed, the higher the interest rate, and the higher your credit score, the lower the interest rate. Keep these factors in mind when you compute for your interest.

When you are shopping around for the best finance rates and dealers, remember to keep looking for better rates elsewhere. RV specialty lenders normally provide very competitive rates, so it is always best to look around instead of going for the first dealer you come across with right away. Just keep in mind that RV motor homes are considered a luxury item, so when you are trying to get your financing in order, finance criteria are very stringent.

Interests paid are **tax deductible** because an RV motorhome is considered a second home. If your RV is considered as one of two residences that you choose for tax deductibility, it must have basic living accommodations such as sleeping, cooking, and bathroom facilities. This also includes freshwater tanks and wastewater tanks. But to make sure, please consult your accountant or CPA.

**Extended warranties on your RV (http://www.rv-dreams.com/rv-insurance.html)**

These kinds of "service contracts" may or may not be issued by the manufacturer, but with a premium or an additional fee, it can provide coverage that extends beyond the period of the manufacturer's own warranty. You are the buyer of the extended service contract, while the contract provider or seller is the company that is responsible for collecting the fee from you and for calculating the quote of the contract. This company is the one that completes the contract application and may be an independent warranty provider, a manufacturer, or a dealer.

The administrator is the one that pays the claims and has the final say on the coverage of the contract. A big chunk of the premium fee goes to the administrator to pay future claims in a claims reserve account. To protect this and to make sure that the claims get paid, you need to be certain of the insurance company's financial status to properly back up your claims reserve account.

## PROS OF GETTING AN EXTENDED WARRANTY

- o An extended warranty eliminates price shocks and surprise costs whenever your RV breaks down and needs repairs. Because typical RV repairs go for approximately $300 per hour, you just might be able to sleep better at night and get some well-deserved peace of mind if you know that you have an extended warranty just in case things go south.

o You can help manage the financial risks of buying an RV with an extended warranty. Your monthly or your annual budget, in general, may not be able to handle skyrocketing costs of replacing air conditioners, refrigerators, transmissions, and other electrical parts, so budget control is one of the biggest advantages of an extended warranty.

o Your extended warranty can act as an emergency fund or a hedge against high prices. You can be insulated against a price increase because the administrator can't ask for more money from you just because of increasing prices in succeeding years.

o An extended service contract can help give you an advantageous edge when you do decide to resell your unit. Your resale value will be better because your extended warranty gives your used buyer additional assurance.

- You won't be able to use your extended service warranty to cover regular maintenance items, pre-existing items, and to cover corrosion, rust, and poor maintenance.

- Your extended service warranty may not cover specialized roadside assistance.

- Your RV motorhome might have too many miles. If your mileage exceeds 80,000 miles or so, most companies will write new contracts to cover this.

- If your RV is too old, keep in mind that there are age limits when it comes to coverage, especially if your RV is already over 10 years old.

## 3 TYPES OF COVERAGE TO LOOK FOR IN AN EXTENDED WARRANTY:

- Exclusionary contract – Always secure a copy of your contract for careful review. With an exclusionary contract, you can cover mechanical aspects of your RV except for anything that is excluded from the coverage as stated in the contract. There can be multiple levels of coverage here, so make sure that you get the one with the most comprehensive coverage.

- Listed component contract – As the name suggests, the coverage includes only what is listed.

- Coach the only contract – This kind of contract covers plenty of components except for the transmission, engine, steering components, and drive axle. It can be the less expensive option if you already have a chassis manufacturer warranty.

- **Value** – Costs of extended warranties may be difficult to justify, but if you know how to shop around and save money, you should be good to go. Just remember that no matter how much the dealer pressures you to get an extended warranty, you should not give in. Most extended warranties mean a big profit for dealers, sometimes even greater than the RV sale itself, which is why they tend to push for the warranties for buyers. Still, when you do decide to get your extended warranty, do not be tempted to get the cheapest one just because of budget constraints. Be cautious of deals that can be too good to be true.

- **Contract protection** – As mentioned previously, you should always do your research and do a background check of the insurance company's financial condition to make sure that your money doesn't just disappear when the need calls for it. Check A-rated insurance companies, and be wary of risk retention groups because they are not that properly regulated.

- o **Flexibility and service** – Whenever your RV breaks down, you want to be able to head on over to the nearest and most convenient repair service facility that is most accessible to you. Also be certain that your contract provider will provide you with after sales services so that they can assist you with your warranty when you do need it.

- o **Deductibles** – Remember that higher deductibles equal lower overall extended warranty price.

- o **Payment of claims and retail costs** – If the administrator makes you pay the repair facility yourself and promises to reimburse your receipts, this can be a warning flag for you. Make sure that your administrator pays the repair facility itself with full retail for parts and labor.

- **Transferability** – Extended warranties should be transferable. This means that you can sell your RV to another buyer whenever you want to in order to increase its resale value.

- **Cancellation terms** – As with any contract, there should be a clear and non-destructive cancellation clause. The cancellation policy, refund policy, initial probation period, pro-rated refunds, and administrative fees for processing the refunds and cancellations must all be clearly stipulated.

- **Additional benefits and add-ons** – Check your extended warranty for emergency repair provisions, roadside assistance, towing benefits, lodging benefits, and the like.

## 6 MUST FOLLOW TIPS AND TRICKS TO GET THE MOST OUT OF YOUR EXTENDED WARRANTY

- To keep yourself sane and to enjoy some peace of mind on your stress-free warranty, you should be able to understand your contract fully and completely. Know your contract inside and out so that you know exactly what you are getting into before you make any purchase decisions. Do not be intimidated by the complex legal terms—get a good lawyer to review your contract if you need to, as this is no simple agreement that you are getting yourself into. Make sure that you understand all of the provisions and that every single term is clear to you. You wouldn't want your claims to get denied right when you need them the most.

- Be aware of everything that is NOT included in your contract. Much like knowing everything you are entitled to in your extended service warranty, you should also be aware of what you ARE NOT getting. This is usually where buyers get confused and frustrated. Just be aware of the things that are not included in your warranty, and find out if you really do need them. If you decide that you do, you can choose to add optional coverage add-ons and be wary of "consequential damage" clauses that may get your claim denied. Always inquire first before making any rash decisions.

- Be absolutely certain that your chosen repair facility gets pre-authorization before you go ahead and ask them to perform any repairs. Look for a repair facility that has a good and extremely well-established warranty department so that you know just the type of personnel to look for when making your claims. Be sure that claiming will be hassle-free with an experienced and very accommodating claims staff.

- Do not expect the administrator to pay for upgrades unless there is an absolutely necessary and well-documented reason to do so. The repairs will only be done when necessary, so do not be surprised if your claims for upgrades will be denied.

- The administrator will inspect your RV properly, so be as accommodating as you can when that happens. The condition for your RV needs to be verified to check if there are any pre-existing damages.

- As much as possible, try not to make a claim immediately after making your extended warranty contract purchase. This is often a suspicious activity for them, because warranty administrators need to be as strict as they can be when it comes to approving and denying claims.

  This is necessary to make sure that all contract holders are protected, and to keep the system in place. There will be an added layer of suspicion and scrutiny if you make a claim soon after your contract purchase, and some might even have waiting periods that you just might violate.

Here's the thing: buying a new RV means that you are buying one that has just been manufactured about a few weeks to a few months earlier. This, of course, is the most expensive way to buy your motorhome. A brand new RV also means that the top of the line RV has a full manufacturer warranty that you can enjoy right off the bat once you buy it, and you will not have any problems or worries about the RV breaking down in the middle of the road for your first travel trip with it.

There are no wear and tear issues, and there is a lot of customizable features that you can choose from at the manufacturer. This includes room layout, color choice, and so much more.

However, buying a fresh and brand new motorhome can be extremely expensive. You might also end up with incurring more expenses down the line because some trailers and RVs are customized elsewhere and not directly through the manufacturer.

There will be high insurance premiums, and you might also have to shell out more hard-earned bucks just to have your brand new trailer shipped to your doorstep.

For used and second-hand RVs, on the other hand, the main advantage is, really, the price. You will be saving a significant amount of money instead of using up a big chunk of it on your initial purchase. You have the option to redecorate, rebuild, or restore your motorhome however way you want to, and, of course, the insurance will also definitely be much cheaper than for brand new motorhomes. You can even pick one that's a classic and one that may not currently be in production anymore.

Still, because it has already been used, you have no idea just what might be wrong with the RV. It might break down for no reason at all or maybe too worn out even on your first road trip.

You also have no way of knowing how long it has been out there since it was first manufactured, and you might end up spending what you thought you saved on repairs and other maintenance costs. The RV has also depreciated over time, and it may not have as great a resell value as it used to have before.

The manufacturer's warranty may also have already run out. When you are buying your very first RV, it is always more prudent to be budget-conscious, but if you have decided to get yourself a used RV, you have absolutely no safety net.

This is why you should always make sure that the person you are buying it from is reputable, or better yet, an actual friend. He or she will be honest with you regarding the condition of the used RV so you will not have any surprise issues once you start using it.

For more information, visit this site:

(http://www.doityourselfrv.com/)

## THE INS AND OUTS OF USED RVS

If you are eying an used or pre-owned RV, or you want to sell your old one, you need to be able to determine what the current RV values in the market are today. It is always important to do your homework before anything else and to begin, you need to calculate the Fair Market Value (FMV) to make sure that you are not underselling your unit or overpaying for a used one.

Unfortunately, buying from someone else who is not the direct dealer means that it may be quite a challenge to identify what the Fair Market Value is, simply because you will not have the same kind of information on the unit as the RV dealer.

To help you out, you can check out the RV Consumer Group (RVCG) and find out the varying RV ratings and data that you will need. The RVCG is a comprehensive information resource for knowledge about the safety, quality, status, average price paid, average list price, expected depreciation schedule, and value of different kinds of RV so that you will know what you are getting yourself into when you do decide to buy a used RV.

One way to find out what the price of an RV should be is to reverse the depreciation on a similar RV. You can find sample computations and templates of the formula in the said RVCG group. You can also make an educated guess as to the value of an RV by keeping in mind that the SRP of a unit usually has as much as 40% markup for dealers depending on the brand of the RV.

You need to research about the current statistics, current market, the condition of your RV, and the like to determine the selling price of an RV. You can also refer to the National Automobile Dealers Association Guides (the NADA Guides) to find out more.

Lastly, if you really want to find out what the realistic expected price of an RV is, you can have it professionally appraised by an RV Appraisal Service. Some insurance companies, lawyers, and manufacturers enlist the services of professional appraisers as well to determine the correct value of a unit, so you know you are in the right hands.

## OTHER COSTS AND EXPENSES YOU NEED TO CONSIDER BEFORE YOU MAKE YOUR PURCHASE

- Gap coverage
- Insurance costs
- Maintenance and repair
- Registration
- Fuel costs and fuel economy (gas costs and propane)
- Internet access
- Cable TV access
- Long-term investment commitment
- Parking during days when you are not on the road
- Storage costs
- Food preparation facilities

- Campsites and where you intend to park on your road trips

# VI. HOW AND WHERE TO BUY YOUR RV

## TIPS AND TRICKS WHEN BUYING YOUR FIRST MOTORHOME

Normally, RVs do not have firm asking prices, unlike cars, do. Some RV dealers may have significant price reductions, while some have big markups from the wholesale prices.

Try to ask for the wholesale price if you can, and make sure that you commission an RV technician to review your choice before buying. Just be wary of dealers negotiating with you on the price of the actual RV and leaving out the negotiations for the add-on amenities and equipment.

The bottom line is to always keep your options open. Do not be pressured into buying the first thing that you see or agreeing on the first price that the first dealer you visit offers you. Regularly check out the auto finance rates from your banks and your dealers, and be patient enough to wait for the good deals to come along.

Usually, you should try to buy your RV during the end of RV season to get better deals, and always be kind, respectful, and friendly to the salesperson who handles your account. Be aware of pricing incentives that come with the hefty tag as well.

(http://www.doityourselfrv.com/rv-buyers-guide-how-buy-rv/5/)

## WHERE DO YOU BUY YOUR RV?

You can choose to either buy your RV online or to buy it locally. Just remember that the humongous advantage of buying your RV locally is that you can see and inspect the actual model right before you before you buy it. You can inspect it physically at the dealer or the RV show, and you can take it for a test drive just to see if it is the right one for you. Still, buying an RV online has better perks and more enticing offers, so you should choose your method wisely.

Either way, the Internet is a great place to do your research before you make the big purchase. Compare prices and manufacturers there to make sure that you get the best deal there is.

## AT AN RV SHOW

After you go through the choices you are considering on the World Wide Web, you may want to visit an RV show to find one that would best fit your budget and your requirements. Talk to the representatives and inquire as much as you can—keep in mind that representatives are usually more than willing to sell you the display RVs rather than have to take them back to their shops. You can even buy the floor models at a significant discount, and if you do your homework and present yourself right, you just might go home with a brand new RV.

## AT A DEALERSHIP

When you are at an RV dealer, remember that all prices can be negotiated. At the end of RV season is the best time to go and buy your RV, as prices will be lower and perks and bundles will come out. Some of the dealers also give better offers and prices for buyers who want to finance with them as well, so always keep that in mind.

## ONLINE PURCHASE

Of course, buying your RV online is the easiest and fastest way to buy an RV. It is quick and overwhelmingly time-saving, and you don't even have to get off your bum while sitting in front of your computer surfing the Net all day. When you are making an online purchase and doing your window shopping, there is an option called "Regionally Available to See before Purchase." This method allows you to narrow down your search parameters to areas that are near to you so that you can test and negotiate your RV at the dealer. Here are some good websites to buy your RV online:

- RV Trader
- eBay
- Camping World
- General RV
- RVT.com

## INDIVIDUAL BUYING PERSONALLY

It's never a good idea to purchase anything from complete strangers, so if you are buying from individual sellers, remember to research the financial history of the model you are eying. Check conditions and terms for state sales tax, title, past ownership, maintenance records, reasons for selling, winterized features, bacteria in the water delivery system, and so on. You should also hire an RV technician to look the model over to inspect for any glaring issues.

## AFTER SALES MATTERS

In buying brand new RVs, the RV show representatives or the particular RV dealer will be the one responsible for handling your registration. On the other hand, buying from an individual private owner means that you are responsible for registering your own unit. Always make sure that you have records of your insurance coverage that you agreed upon with your dealer, especially during delivery as well.

As for the government taxes, most states will require you to pay your taxes at registration. RV show representatives or RV dealers will usually handle this for you as well. Here's an additional tip—if you are curious about tax breaks, consult with your tax advisor about deductions for loan interest because of your second home. Plus, since you will be traveling around and can virtually be at home in any state, you need to discuss state tax requirements with your tax advisor as well.

## HOME BASE MATTERS

What is a home base? This kind of thing might seem like a complicated matter, but you don't have to be intimidated by the complex legal system. In the United States, you can be considered as a U.S. citizen, but this also means that you need to be a citizen of a certain state. This state is where you need to establish legal residency, which will also be your official home base.

Keep in mind that the legal domicile is different from your residency because residency is considered more temporary as you can have many residences. By contrast, you can only have a single legal domicile. To determine the place that you can consider your legal domicile, you have to be able to "intend" to establish your legal domicile there. Despite that term, the mere intent to establish domicile will not suffice, as you need to prove that intent by declaring significant contacts in that state.

The problem arises when fulltime RV aficionados essentially live everywhere and wherever the road takes them, so the state needs to look for places where you work, where you own some property, where your voter registration is, where your driver's license and will is registered, and where your vehicles are registered.

Issues like this might have to be clarified in court to establish where your legal domicile actually is. Just be wary about establishing your contacts and your legal residence, as you might end up paying taxes in varying states without any clear rules. You have to factor in details like your income tax, property taxes, vehicle registration, insurance matters, and your own personal convenience.

When we talk about convenience, this usually means that you establish your "contacts" as a full-timer in a state where you previously live, or in the state where you grew up, have family members in, or lived many years prior. This means that you are familiar with the administration of taxes and legal documents in that area. Some full-timers, however, choose their home base by considering the various state income tax requirements in a particular state.

These can range from .07% to approximately 13.3%, with states such as Alaska, Nevada, Florida, South Dakota, Washington, Wyoming, and Texas having none.

This does not mean that you should immediately go for states with no income tax, because sometimes, choosing a state with minimal income tax on low income may be a more prudent choice because some states may have higher insurance premiums.

## PROPERTY TAXES AND VEHICLE REGISTRATION

Because personal property taxes can be complicated with its variations on different states, you need to compare your options as thoroughly as you can. Some states charge personal property taxes, while some states do not. The amounts of these taxes can pile up and amount to a great deal of money toward the end of the year, because taxes can be charged on your RV value, the value of your towable vehicle, or your tow vehicle itself. You can check out the different taxes for these in different states on the Internet, but make sure that you do so in the jurisdiction of your vehicle registration.

Speaking of the registration of your vehicle, these can also vary by city and state. You need to properly and thoroughly check for the different state requirements for registration and licensing. There can be annual vehicle safety inspections as well as emissions inspections, and some of them can be done conveniently online so that you will not have to go to the administration yourself every single year.

## INSURANCE AND HOME BASE ISSUES

All based on the state of your domicile, health insurance, life insurance, vehicle insurance, and RV insurance undergo complicated actuarial science to determine the exact mathematical computations and statistics for underwriting. The various claims on these rates are identified by state, zip code, and the like. Keep in mind that you should consider these factors, as well as your own health insurance from the state, when you choose your home base.

# VII. MOST POPULAR RV BRANDS

## AIRSTREAM

If you want your recreational vehicle to be all about the luxury, then Airstream is the brand to go to. The Airstream brand has steadily produced some of the most iconic and the most distinctive styles in the market today, and as such, the Airstream models are usually the ones that are priced on the travel trailer price range near the high end.

Still, because of the hefty price tag, you can at least be certain that the model you are buying is fully equipped with the best and most top of the line amenities in terms of price value and superior craftsmanship. You can also rest assured that your purchase will stand the test of time, and will be durable enough for all the long haul road trips you are planning to take with your family and friends.

## GRAND DESIGN

A break off from Keystone, Grand Design boasts of its fabulous designs and excellent customer service—the 3 Year limited structural warranty on all coaches alone is a testimony to this.

## FOREST RIVER

With multiple production plants located on the west coast and throughout the midwest, the Forest River brand produces quality recreational vehicles based on the vision of its founder Peter Liegl Forest River when the company began its operations in 1996. Its travel trailers, fifth wheelers, pop-up campers, and so much more are guaranteed to provide safe and durable transportation for happy customers and RV owners.

## GULFSTREAM

Because this brand has been around since 1983, Gulfstream knows how to provide outstanding quality and state of the art innovation for its customers. It has since then been well known in the industry among RV owners in the community.

## HEARTLAND

Heartland is located in Elkhart, Indiana and was founded by Brian Brady and company in 2003. Well loved by consumers and owners of travel trailers everywhere, the Heartland model has come to be one of the most popular brands in the RV industry today.

## ECLIPSE RECREATIONAL VEHICLES

Also founded in 2003, Eclipse Recreational Vehicles prides itself as one of the biggest and most popular producers of toy haulers and travel trailers, spanning over 50 models of varying kinds.

## JAYCO

Who has not heard of the Jayco brand in the RV community? The time and the tested brand have been around since 1968. Founded by Lloyd J. Bontrager, the Jayco brand is unique among the rest as it mixes Old World Amish craftsmanship with creative and modern innovative technology to bring RV owners quality and comfort. It is no wonder that the Jayco brand is the country's largest family-owned RV manufacturer right now.

## WINNEBAGO

Another well-known and instant classic, the Winnebago is so popular in its brand that it has become a household name in RV motorhomes for both owners and non-owners alike. It has a rich and colorful history of over 50 years in the travel trailer industry, and its motorhomes are instantly at the top of anyone's mind whenever the topic on travel trailers pops up.

## LA MESA RV

What began as a little single dealership in 1972 has now grown into a multiple dealership companies, with dealerships in Florida, Arizona, California, and New Mexico. The company sells a wide range of brand new and second hand RVs and trailers, so if you are in the market for pre-owned RVs, then La Mesa RV might be a great place to start.

## THOR INDUSTRIES

It is important to note that Thor Industries acquired Airstream in 1980, and now also owns RV brands like General Coach and Jayco.

## FLEETWOOD RV

Diligently manufacturing motorhomes since 1950, Fleetwood RV boasts of its quality Class A and Class C motorhomes for both gas and diesel options. It is part of the REV Group, and the company also allows you to customize your chosen motorhome with plenty of various options.

## NEWMAR

if you fancy attention to detail and high luxury, Newmar is the brand to go with. The company has been manufacturing excellent RVs since 1968, and the high-end luxury models only prove that the family-owned RV brand values your comfort, elegance, and pure sophistication no matter where you go.

Based in Indiana, the company aims to create the best coaches on the road, as committed by founders Marvin Newcomer and Marvin Miller. The Amish workmanship is a great unique quality and adds to the company's passion for being advocates of RV quality work.

## PREVOST

Since 1924, the Prevost Company has been creating bus shells, luxury RVs, and touring coaches and offered services for specialty conversions as well. You can customize your chosen motorhome to meet your needs and specifications, as well as convert the shells so that everything will suit your own refined and particular tastes.

## NEWELL COACH RV

Newell is one of the top manufacturers of some of the best and most luxurious RV motorhomes in the industry, Newell Coach RV will definitely cost you some big bucks. However, this company based in Miami, Oklahoma will make sure that every penny is worth it, as the coaches and travel homes have quite luxurious amenities that you most likely will not find anywhere else.

Because the company only produces approximately 24 coaches every year, their RVs are usually the most wanted and most sought after products in the industry. RV motor homeowners include Roger Penske, Matt Kenseth, Jimmie Johnson, and Dale Earnhardt.

In 2010, Nu Wa Industries revolutionized its role in the industry by letting customers purchase directly from the factory, which is a choice that many RV motor homeowners have come to enjoy and appreciate. Known for producing some of the best fifth wheels in the industry, Nu Wa Industries is the brand responsible for the ever popular Hitchhiker. Innovative, creative, modern, and bold, the brand is one of the most highly reviewed brands in the market today.

## PLEASURE-WAY

For those who are looking for custom Class B motorhomes, Pleasure-Way lets customers choose from their base builds from completed Chevrolet, Ford, and Mercedes chassis. Pleasure-Way received the Gold Readers' Choice Award from Motorhome Magazine in 2014 and has since then been a top competitor for luxury and quality craftsmanship.

Despite being a small company, Tiffin Motor Homes prides itself in the personal touch that it grants its customers. The company places a great deal of value on getting to know its customers, its people, and its relationships more than it values its bottom line—something that not a lot of big RV motorhome companies can provide.

## OTHERS

Overall, the type of RV motorhome and brand that you choose will ultimately depend on your budget and your particular tastes. Still, a few other brands include:

- Coachmen RV: travel trailers, fifth wheels, toy haulers, motorhomes
- Dutchmen RV:  Aerolite, Aspen Trail, Coleman, Denali, Kodiak, Razorback, Rubicon, Voltage
- Trillium Travel Trailers – Fiberglass travel trailers, Ultralite lightweight tow
- Scamp Travel Trailers – Fiberglass travel trailers

- Keystone RV: fifth wheel recreational vehicles, ultra-lightweight travel trailers, towables, fifth luxury wheels
- Shasta RV –travel trailers and fifth wheels
- Starcraft –AR-One, travel trailers, toy haulers, fifth wheels
- T@B – teardrop travel trailers
- Little Guy – T@B, My Pod M@X, T@G, Ultralite travel trailers, teardrop styles
- Lance Camper –travel trailers, campers, toy haulers, dry-baths in Ultralite travel trailers, medium weights
- Northwood Manufacturing - travel trailers, fifth wheels, lightweights, truck campers, toy haulers, Artic Fox, Nash, SnowRiver, Wolf Creek, Desert Fox, Fox Mountain

When you are dealing with the varying brands, types, and models of the various RV motorhomes, it is important to do some extensive research as most brands will have their own loyal following.

You can check out plenty of forums, threads, and exclusive Facebook groups and follow the users and owners on social media platforms just so you can get a sense of the pros and cons of every type and brand, and so that you can see how the owners are using and maintaining their units.

There can be a loyal following for a particular brand which makes it a popular choice among the community, but if it ultimately doesn't sit too well with you, then you should keep researching until you find the proverbial "The One." Check out some of these websites for more information on the various RV motorhome brands:

- https://www.consumeraffairs.com/automotive/rv-manufacturers/
- https://blog.carsforsale.com/comparison-of-top-10-rv-brands/
- https://topratedtraveltrailers.com/10-best-travel-trailer-brands/
- https://www.outdoorsy.co/blog/the-big-guide-to-rv-manufacturers/

# VIII. THE NEXT LEVEL: UPGRADING YOUR RV ON A BUDGET

To make any road trip more enjoyable, you can choose from a variety of add-ons and accessories for your RV motorhome—things that you can easily purchase and transport wherever your destination may be.

## ACCESSORIES AND OTHER ADD-ONS FOR YOUR RV MOTORHOME

### PORTABLE MEAT SMOKERS

One of the most amazing and most enjoyable beauties of the great outdoors is the fact that you can fire up the grill and cook outside anytime you feel like it. With portable meat smokers, you can cook up a storm whenever you like without having to worry about how your smokers will fit into small cramped spaces.

These portable meat smokers can easily be carried and transported along with you on your road trip with your friends so that you and your best buds can pop open a cold can of your favorite beer and enjoy some smoked grub while enjoying the beauty of nature. You can grill, smoke, roast, or bake all kinds of food to satisfy even the most particular of your carnivorous pals out there.

## FLAMELESS BATTERY OPERATED CANDLES

Speaking of cooking outdoors, more often than not, you will encounter a situation wherein you will need to cook under the moonlight. Flameless battery operated candles can come in handy when you need some extra lighting during the darkest of nights when you are cooking outside, and because they are battery operated, you will not have to worry about any matches getting wet.

## MOBILE WI-FI HOTSPOT

Just because you are traveling the great outdoors does not mean that you need to be remotely isolated from the outside world with no contact with anyone else. With a mobile Wi-Fi hotspot, you can take the World Wide Web along with you so that you can check up on your emails, your social media apps, and your family and friends while on the road.

## CAST IRON COOKWARE

Perfectly ideal for camping, cast iron cookware are sturdy, durable, and highly reliable for when you are on the road and have limited cooking materials to use over an open fire. This type of cookware will not have any risk of damage and is the best bet for some quick grub outside.

## FOLDABLE BIKES

Fancy a quick ride on the road with your kids? Space is usually a problem for common RVs, but with foldable bikes, you can attach them to the back of your RV or fold them up and secure them inside when not needed.

## INSECT REPELLENT

A camping and outdoor essential, the insect repellant is your number one weapon against pesky mosquitoes threatening to ruin your fabulous trip outdoors. You never know when insects are prevalent, and this handy item will keep those annoyingly itchy bites from spoiling your good time.

## WATERPROOF LIGHTER

Another outdoor cooking essential, the waterproof lighter will not only help you fire up your cooking game when you are grilling or smoking outdoors, but it will also help you build fires whenever it is damp and raining outside with no problem at all. You can even use the waterproof lighter to light a wire during windy days with wind strengths of up to 8mph.

## RV SATELLITE DISH AND MUSIC

Some people cannot live without their favorite TV shows on cable, and since the RV motorhome is, in fact, your home on wheels, why not purchase and carry a mobile RV satellite dish with you? You can easily set it up and hook it up so that you can get some decent reception for days when long stretches of the road become a bore and when you desperately need to catch that weekly TV series you have been following religiously since Season 1.

Even better is when you pack up and bring all of your music with you, because who wants to drive along a long and winding road without some tunes? You can even belt out at the top of your lungs and have a-rockin' karaoke party with your family and friends. Simply load up some road trip music and travel in style with your favorite melodies with you. And if you want to go the next level, why not bring along a guitar with you too?

## COMFY OUTDOOR SEATS

Chairs and loungers are an absolute must when traveling because you never know when you might need to kick back and relax outside for a quick break. There is nothing worse than wanting to lounge around in the perfect weather outside and not having anything to sit on but muddy rocks and sharp edges. Your mobile home and your whole road trip should be all about the rest and relaxation, and lounge chairs are a crucial part of that experience!

## CARDS, GAMES, AND ENTERTAINMENT

Eventually, the long road trip will reach a point when everything becomes monotonous and boring. There is no boredom that a deck of cards and a good set of board games can't fix, especially when the rainy days come and there is no way for anyone to step outside. Being cooped up indoors all day does not have to be about the gloom and doom—just set up those pieces and cards and you will definitely get distracted from the heavy downpour outside.

## FIRST AID KIT

In any given travel situation, you should make like the Boy Scouts and always be prepared. A trusty and complete First Aid Kit will keep you and your family and friends safe from sudden cuts, emergency injuries, and common infections. Nothing dampens a road trip party more than a cut, a scratch, a bee sting, and other injuries that otherwise would have been comforted by some Band-Aid strips and some antibacterial cream.

## EMERGENCY REPAIR KIT

Just like the first aid kit, you will need to pack essential repair tools like extra batteries, chargers, duct tape, work gloves, a shovel, a small axe, some silicone rescue tape, a Swiss army knife, cords and clothes, extra clothes, a bucket, electrical tape and spare fuses, and the like. These—on top of a sound and calm mind— will save you during a small crisis, so do not scrimp on them when you have some extra space in your RV!

# IX. PROPER CARE AND MAINTENANCE FOR YOUR RV WHEN YOU ARE NOT ON THE ROAD

## PROTECTING YOUR RV MOTOR HOME

As with any important purchase, you want to make sure that you make your investment last as long as you possibly can. Especially with big purchases like an RV motorhome, extending its lifespan is crucial so that you can enjoy the spoils of your labor for a good long while. To do that, you need to be able to give your RV some ample protection, and you need to spend for its upkeep and maintenance as well as opposed to just letting it rot in the back yard.

Keep those leakages and regular wear and tear at bay with these helpful tips and tricks:

1. Invest in a portable RV garage to keep your travel trailer nice and protected. An example would be the Shelter Logic Garage-in-a-Box. Just make sure that your portable garage has the right length for your whole RV, and if you need to add some extra height, you can build a platform for it if needed.

2. Build a shed or a pole barn for your RV if needed. You can get yourself some reclaimed materials to save up on tools and equipment too.

3. If you purchased a second-hand or pre-owned travel trailer, you could caulk the outside of your RV to help seal it up and keep those pesky leakages at bay when the rains come.

4. Build a deck for your RV for some much needed outside living space. This deck can also double as a frame for your RV garage. Do not forget to get yourself a good, quality doormat to keep the dirt at bay. Nothing ruins a good clean home than a pair of dirty shoes tracking mud all over your precious and newly cleaned floor!

5. Invest in some sturdy camping chairs. When you are chilling outside or taking a break from the long and tiresome drive, you will want to lay out a few lounge chairs outside so that you can kick back and relax in peace. Good camping chairs will also come in handy when you have a

few guests coming over, or when you are hosting a particularly crowded barbecue party outside your RV motorhome. You are going to want to stay calm and cool and chill out with them outside, and you can't have a nice chat with your guests if they have nowhere to sit.

6. Get yourself some sufficient storage space. There is a whole lot of outdoor stuff that you will be needing when you finally hit the long and open road. You are going to need gallons and gallons of clean water jugs, some propane tanks, and a great deal of outdoor stuff. You can invest in a portable RV garage to help with all the storage space you are definitely going to need.

## OF POWER REQUIREMENTS AND OTHER ELECTRICITY NEEDS

Your RV mobile home will not really be as mobile if you are hooked up to a power grid all the time. Chances are, with you traveling everywhere in your RV, you are going to need some sort of power source solution such as a solar power source or a portable generator.

1. Look for and purchase a quality power generator. A good recommendation is a 3000-watt power generator for all of your electricity needs. This way, you have more than enough electricity to power your RV, as long as you use up a couple of hours every single day to recharge your power generator properly. Look for a generator that is lightweight and totally mobile so that it will not be a hassle to carry it around with you wherever your road trip or outdoor journey takes you.

2. Get yourself a battery charger. Most trailers have what is called a trickle charger, and it just might take you more than 8 hours every single day just to charge the battery. You might end up draining the battery faster than you can charge it, and to keep that from happening, you can use a battery charger to charge your battery directly to make recharging fast and efficient.

3. Shop around for some high quality LED lights. You can reduce your power consumption a great

deal simply by switching your lights to LED ones. Just make sure that you buy the really good ones instead of the cheap versions, as you just might end up wasting your precious and hard earned money on less expensive LED lights, thinking you are saving up when you are really just wasting your money. Upgrade to higher quality ones—they are much brighter and can last so much longer, making them completely worth the added cost.

4. Just like I mentioned earlier, you need to have a good, reliable, and cost-efficient power source, such as a solar source for electricity. To do this, get yourself some portable solar panels. This will help you cut down on your electricity costs especially during the summer season when days are long, and the sun is scorching hot. You should make the most of what nature provides, after all!

## BLACK WATER AND SEPTIC ISSUES

Disgusting, gross, and a bit of a headache, black water is the stuff that comes down from the toilet, and it can be quite a hassle to deal with. Depending on your family usage, you may have to dispose of your black water anywhere from between every five days to about every seven days. You should also be wary of spending too much on your toilet paper consumption, as well as getting your valves clogged with chunks and chunks of toilet paper wads. For men, you can opt to pee outside if you can to save up for toilet time.

Be absolutely sure that you empty out your black water completely whenever you feel the need to do so. Also, you should fill up the tank completely before you decide to dump it so that you can keep those stinky odors at bay and keep your tank clean as well.

Note that your sensors may sometimes get blocked and may not work, creating false indications of the status of your septic tank. Solid waste can build upon it and cause it to malfunction, so be sure to perform regular maintenance on it too. You can pour some bleach down the toilet to keep things sanitized if you like.

## WHEN YOU ARE RENTING AN RV

Renting may be the cheaper option as compared to buying an RV, but there can also be sticker shock for you when you rent for the very first time. Most RV dealers and some car rental agencies can allow you to rent RV motorhomes, and some of the more reputable ones are Cruise America and El Monte RV.

You can set up a reservation via the World Wide Web or over the phone, choose your preferred model, place your deposit, and go rent. Here's a pro tip: do not simply choose the largest RV on the lot when you choose your model to rent. Consider all the different factors like flexibility, mobility, and other things. You just might be surprised with how little you can live by on the road.

If you are traveling with other people, try to bring them all along with you on your test drive of the model you are thinking about renting. Make sure everyone is comfortable with the chosen model before you make your decision.

Do not over pack, and learn to read the materials and instructions on how to get started with your rented RV. If you are a seasoned driver, do not assume that you already know everything there is to know about driving. Handling an RV can be completely different from handling other vehicles, and you will need to re-learn the basics from start to finish. You should also be very aware of every single thing that is happening around you in your surroundings, whether you are parked comfortably in an area or driving down the open road. Do not be in a rush, as you are handling a large vehicle.

Just drive at your own pace, and you can enjoy the leisure that RV driving offers you. Know how to switch lanes, park, go up hills, and the like. You need to be able to adjust to RV driving, and be able to handle situations like drawers popping out and other things clunking around in there while you are driving.

And while we are at it, do not simply just wing it. Driving an RV is no joke, and is no simple matter. Planning every single issue ahead of time saves you from going through a mental and emotional breakdown when something untoward does happen while you are out on the wide and open road.

Learn how to plan your budget, and how much you want to allocate for food, entertainment options, overnight stays, eating outside in restaurants, routes to take, and stops that you want to see along the way.

You should learn to create a campground checklist, to make sure that everyone is following the proper routine on the road. Here are the many things that you should consider on your campground:

- Low hanging branches

- Electrical, water, sewage, and other obstacles on the ground
- Blocks and stabilizing jocks
- Electrical hookups
- Sewer hoses and rain hookups
- Awnings and campsite set-ups
- Date codes on your tires to determine how old the wheels are and to be prepared for tire breakdown (the tread should be replaced for a recommended period of every 5 to 7 years)
- Planning your routes, stops, and sight-seeing in advance

## CAMPING OPTIONS AND CAMPSITES

For newbies and RV newcomers, most RV parks and campgrounds can be open and available with rent spaces for nightly and weekly rates. The prices can range from $15 to around $50 every night, and some parks may even charge $10 or have free rental spaces.

Take note that some rental spaces do not have utility hookups, so be sure to check and research the campgrounds online. You can also join RV clubs like Good Sam Club and Passport America to get member discounts and insider information on the various camp grounds all over the country.

Have you ever heard of boondocking, wild camping, or dry camping? You can put your RV motorhome to good use as well if you do decide to camp outside of designated campgrounds.

Road trippers can then camp in public areas with no cost or charge, but while it sounds simple enough, there are a variety of factors you need to consider before going through with it. Boondocking or dry camping means camping without hookups, and as such, there are many things to consider, such as the pros and cons and various limitations of your camping experience.

Your particular RV may have its own limitations when it comes to dry camping.

For instance, if you have a smaller sized RV, then options for your campsite are more flexible, whereas if you have a bigger sized RV, it may be more difficult to maneuver your vehicle around and find a good place to camp without hookups.

Still, having a smaller RV also means that you will have limitations on storage space, resources, limited capacity, batteries, gray water and black water, and the like. It might be more difficult for you to make electricity especially since you have limited or no hookups.

When you have properly determined the limitations and capabilities of your RV, think long and hard about your needs, comfort level, and your non-negotiables. You may have to sacrifice some modern conveniences and luxuries, so it is crucial to identify which requirements for you are the most important, and which ones are negligible.

You need to know how to balance these things properly, and as you gain more experience regarding dry camping, you will find it easier to determine the things you can let go and the things that you absolutely must have on your trip.

Since you are dry camping with the bare necessities, fresh water is one of the most important things that you need to take into consideration. If you are conservative with your fresh water, you can survive out there for longer periods of time—not to mention that being conservative with your water will also reduce the rate of how fast your gray water tank will fill up.

To preserve your fresh water for a longer period of time, you can utilize a plastic dishpan when you shower. This will help capture the water that you are using to keep it from going completely to waste.

You can then use the water that you have captured in that plastic dishpan for washing the dishes, doing some quick and light laundry, flushing the toilet, and so much more. You can also get yourself a dump cap with a hose fitting, and a garden hose so that you can attach them to each other and use the gray water to spray bushes and water plants.

You can collect your rinse water and your dishwater and pour them over plants.

Whenever you shower, you very quickly use up your fresh water and fill up your gray water tank as well. To learn more on the conservative side, you can go for an alternative solution to save water by using a solar shower.

Lay it out in the sun for a few hours, and you will instantly have a hot shower, and you can even get yourself some extra water supply too.

Keep in mind that since your black water tank holds all of your gross toilet waste, you cannot dump it just anywhere. You should dump your black water tank contents in a proper dump station or proper disposal. You can also make use of a built-in cassette toilet with a removable tank that is accessible via an outside compartment door.

There is a great deal of convenience that you can experience here, as the toilet can be emptied out into any toilet, which is a good advantage if you have regular access to toilets.

As for your electrical concerns, you can still use your appliances if you are hooked to shore power with access to 120 volt and 12-volt power. With a limited 12 power source when you are off the grid, however, you can only have limited access to appliances, which excludes your air conditioner and your microwave.

Most likely, you will only have access to your fridge, lights, and your water pump with a 12-volt system operation, so RV batteries are extremely important.

Here are a few ways you can conserve electricity, especially during the times when you have limited access to outlets and power. As usual, you can turn off all of the appliances and lights when you are not using them, and only turn on your appliances and lights one at a time. Use battery operated lights and tools whenever you can, or, if you have the necessary materials, equipment, and resources, you can install some solar panels to use up solar power on bright sunny days.

Because using the sun to charge up your equipments and collect electrical energy is low maintenance, has no moving parts, and does not make a great deal of noise like a traditional generator does, it is an extremely effective way to save up on costs.

Finally, one of the biggest costs you might have when you are dry camping is the use of propane or gas. Your liquid propane gas system is more often than not already built into your RV motorhome, and this kind of handy dandy system will be quite useful for heating hot water, operating refrigerators, and running cook tops for preparing meals.

Two tanks can last you weeks and months depending on your particular usage, so make sure that you plan your trip accordingly. It is important to know how many of you are going on the trip, and how much food and heat you need to prepare and generate on a daily basis.

Much like the calculations on the solar panels and matching the solar power you need to the various appliances you might want to power up, knowing how much you will be using your propane will determine how many tanks of your liquid propane gas system you will be carrying on board with you on your dry camping journey.

That being said, just remember to plan wisely, and most of all, enjoy your trip! A world of dry camping adventure awaits!

# X. MISCELLANEOUS RV TERMS AND GLOSSARY

Now that you know everything there is to know about living the RV motorhome life, it is time to test your knowledge and see just how well you will fit into the wonderful world of RV-ing! Learn how to talk like a legitimate RV-er as a warm welcome to this brave new world of living life on the wide and open road of pure pleasure and freedom.

With this quick glossary from Thor Industries, check out some of the most common terms that you will most likely encounter on the road as you begin your journey.

- Axle Ratio – This refers to the number of revolutions that is needed for the axle to be turned once. Keep in mind that the higher the ratio here, the higher the torque and towing power.
- Auxiliary Battery – This is the extra battery that you keep on board with you so that you can power some 12 Volt appliances.

- Arctic Package – You can set up an RV for winter by adding heat strips on holding tanks, adding insulation, and adding storm windows for good winterization.
- Anode Rod – The anode rod is the component of the water heater that draws things that cause corrosion away from the metal tank.
- Adjustable Ball Mount – This lets you adjust the hitch ball and fine tune it so that you can ensure that your tow vehicle is leveled.
- Bypass Valve – The Bypass valve helps you divert the fresh water from passing through your water heater.
- Bumper-mount Hitch – This type of ball hitch can be attached to the bumper of the tow vehicle, or can be mounted.
- Break-away System – If for any reason, the RV breaks away from the tow vehicle (perhaps due to a hitch failure of some sort), and this device will automatically activate the brakes of a towable RV.
- Brake Actuator/Controller – Mounted on the tow vehicle, this electronic device can control the brakes of the towable RV.

- Backup Monitor – This camera is installed on the back of an RV and connects to a digital monitor so that you can, as the driver, get a better view of the objects behind you, especially when reversing or towing.
- Blue boy – This refers to the portable waste handling tank, named as such because this comes in a blue plastic tank.
- Condensation – Condensation is the term used to refer to the moisture that builds up when the warm air hits the cold window glass of your RV. You can keep condensation to a minimum by opening a roof vent.
- Cargo Carrying Capacity (CCC) – The CCC refers to the allowable weight that your towable RV can handle.
- Camber – The camber refers to the degree of which the wheel is off the vertical measurement. When the tops of the wheel are farther apart than the bottom ones, then positive camber happens. Negative camber, on the other hand, can happen when the RV carries heavier loads.
- Cab-over or over-cab – This is the portion of the RV that can extend above the top of the cab of

your tow vehicle, and this can include a sleeping area as well.

- DSI Ignition – When you light up the burner of an appliance that is fueled by propane, then you use a DSI Ignition. You can use this to power up your water heater, your furnace, your stove, or your fridge.

- Doughnut/Sewer Doughnut – Used to seal the dump hose of the RV to the campsite's sewer hookup, this rubber ring keeps unwanted odors and gases from escaping.

- Equalizing Hitch/Weight-distributing Hitch – This specialized hitch can redistribute the hitch weight of the RV.

- Gross Vehicle Weight Rating (GVWR) – This refers to the maximum allowable operating weight of your RV. This may include the holding tanks, the passengers themselves, your various gear, and your fuel and propane.

- Hitch Weight – Ideally between 10-25% of your towable RV's total weight, the hitch weight is the weight placed on your towing hitch.

- Heat Exchanger – The heat exchanger uses propane flame and ignition devices in order to transform fuel into heat.

- Occupant and Cargo Carrying Capacity (CCC) – Including occupants and passengers, the CCC is the allowable weight that your RV motorhome can carry.
- Overflow Area – often times during peak seasons, most standard RV campsites might already be taken and occupied. In such cases, you can head on over to the overflow area, which is the portion of the campground that includes fewer hookups and amenities.
- Pull-Through – The pull-through is a kind of campground or campsite that lets your RV enter from one end and exit from the other side. This kind of campground is pretty useful for larger sized RVs that may have a hard time backing up out of the campsite.
- Tow Rating – The tow rating refers to the maximum capacity or the biggest permissible weight that your vehicle is allowed to tow.
- Thermocouple – If you have an appliance that is fueled by propane, the thermocouple helps you monitor that pilot flame by shutting the gas valve to stop propane flow when the pilot goes out.

- Unloaded Vehicle Weight (UVW)/Dry Weight/Curb Weight – This refers to the RV weight as an RV is manufactured from the factory. This curb weight or dry weight may include all the weight that is placed on the axle of an RV, as well as on the hitch if it is a towable RV. This UVW can also include fluids required during operation, which can include coolants, generator fluids, engine oil, fuels, and other things.

That's just the tip of the iceberg! More and more exciting new adventures are in store for you, now that you're prepped and ready to start RV-ing. Even after reading this guide, there are some things that you can only learn through experience, so go on out there and get started!

(https://www.thorindustries.com/getting-started/glossary/)

# BEFORE YOU HIT THE ROAD
## RV Maintenance Checklist

### Appliances

- ☒ Refrigerator
- ☒ Inspect door seals
- ☒ Inspect burner flame
- ☒ Clean thermocouple tip
- ☒ Clean area behind refrigerator
- ☒ Furnace
- ☒ Check blower
- ☒ Check combustion chamber
- ☒ Check control compartment
- ☒ Inspect gas line
- ☒ Air conditioning unit
- ☒ Clean air filters
- ☒ Clean condensing unit
- ☒ Check voltage
- ☒ Hot water heater
- ☒ Flush every 6 months
- ☒ Clean burner tube
- ☒ Inspect sacrificial electrode
- ☒ Stove
- ☒ Make sure it produces blue flames
- ☒ Clear vents of animal nests and debris

### Walkaround

- ☒ Inspect roof/body for cracks
- ☒ Check all lights and turn signals
- ☒ Check gas levels in propane tanks
- ☒ Charged fire extinguisher
- ☒ Test smoke detectors
- ☒ Test carbon monoxide detectors

### General Maintenance

Check:
- ☒ Engine oil
- ☒ Transmission oil
- ☒ Tire pressure
- ☒ Tire wear
- ☒ Battery
- ☒ Brake fluid
- ☒ Power steering fluid
- ☒ Engine belts
- ☒ Engine coolant
- ☒ Windshield washer fluid

### Plumbing

- ☒ Check that water pump flows well
- ☒ Flush waste tanks
- ☒ Inspect valves and water pump for leaks
- ☒ Inspect connection dump hose and fittings
- ☒ Sanitize water system

Made in the USA
San Bernardino, CA
18 December 2017